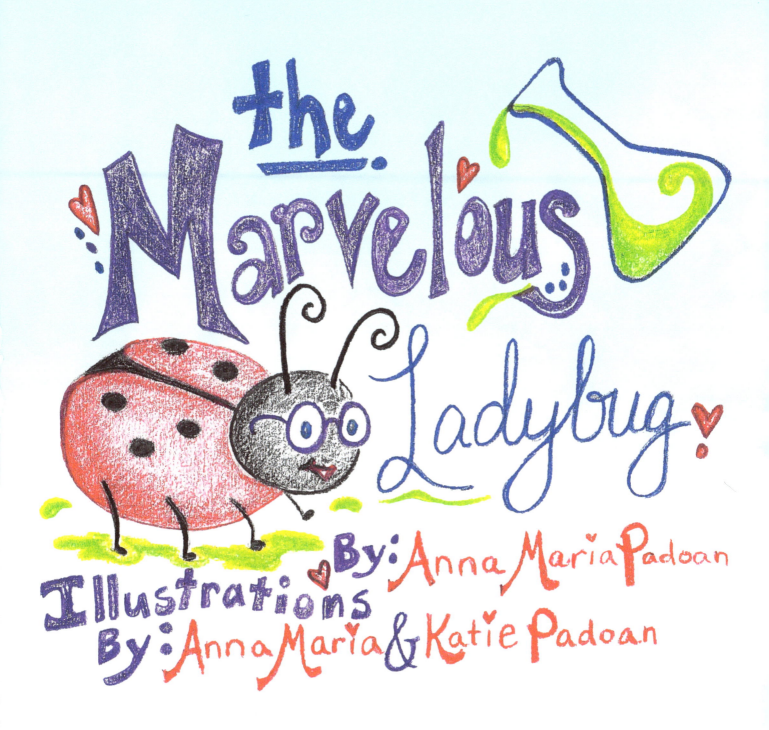

Copyright © 2021 by Anna Maria Padoan and Christopher A. Padoan

All Rights Reserved. This literary work may not be reproduced or transmitted in any form or by any means, including electronic or photographic reproduction, in whole or in part, without express written permission.

All characters and events in this book are fictitious. Any resemblance to actual persons living or dead is strictly coincidental.

Title: **The Marvelous Ladybug**

Author: Anna Maria Padoan

Printed in the United States of America

ISBN: 978-1-716-15350-1

Dedication and Credits

I dedicate this book to the children of the World. Hope they enjoy the adventures and survival of *THE MARVELOUS LADYBUG*.

Special thanks to my Mom, Pop Pop and my extended family for their support and encouragement throughout the process.

Daddy was also helpful by teaching me how to stay within the approved family budget.

Once upon a time,
there was a family of four.
There was a mother,
a father, and two sisters.

$$\text{Growth Rate} = \left(\frac{\text{present}}{\text{past}}\right)^{1/n} - 1$$

The father was
a world-renowned scientist
who was working on
a growth formula.

One time, when the family went to the park, a ladybug flew into Father's workshop and landed on a table.

It was crawling around when, suddenly,
a gust of wind blew the father's formula over,
spilling it onto the table. The ladybug was right
there in the puddle of formula!

The ladybug didn't mind and kept walking. It was a hot summer's day and the liquid felt cool and refreshing.

And then
BOOM!
The ladybug was bigger than ever.

When the family arrived home,
they went on with their day.
Mother began making dinner and the girls helped her.

Father went into his shop to do some work and screamed, "AHHH!"

The rest of the family was very worried because they had never heard Father scream before.

They rushed into the workshop and froze with their mouths and eyes opened wide.

Father was playing catch with a ginormous ladybug. It was nearly as big as he was!

NO PETS
Allowed in this HOUSEHOLD!

Father explained that he screamed not out of fear, but because he had ALWAYS wanted a pet. He realized the ladybug could be his pet... and a special one at that. Mother was so angry you could see smoke coming out of her ears.

Father and the children turned their attention to her. They knew it was not a good sign.

Mother yelled, "No pets allowed in this household!"

Father explained that if they kept the ladybug,
they would be rich!
Mother thought about it a moment and said…. "Ok!"

The family became extremely popular because of the giant ladybug.

They were treated so well they thought they were royalty. Father felt like a king, Mother felt like a queen, and the two sisters felt like beautiful princesses.

But as the months went by, it was still a mystery how the ladybug had become so big.

Father did some tests
and he discovered
it was his formula...

HOORAY!

The family became so famous that people all over the world knew their names.

Eventually, the girls moved away to live on their own while Father and Mother cared for the ladybug.

The family agreed that when the girls turned 40, they would come and live with the ladybug. Mother and Father wanted to retire and be free to dine at all-you-can-eat buffets where they could try EVERYTHING. **Yum! Yum!**

Finally, the girls turned 40 and they were so excited!
They hurried to their mother and father's house.
But when they arrived, they found that
things had become very weird.

The ladybug had gotten bigger and bigger
until it was larger than the house!

Father was concerned at how fast the ladybug was growing. He thought if he didn't give it a shrink formula fast, they would be doomed. He determined the ladybug would explode at sundown!

For the rest of the day, Father worked and worked and worked until finally he finished making the shrink formula.

However, the ladybug was nowhere to be found.
Father said, "Oh no! If I don't give the ladybug
this shrink formula soon, we will be destroyed!"
He finally spotted the ladybug in the distance eating
a giant oak tree. The sun was going down and
he knew he couldn't reach the ladybug in time.

He ran as fast as he could toward the ladybug.
It was nighttime now and he couldn't see anything,
so he threw the bottle with all might
in the hope of hitting the ladybug.

The bottle sailed into the dark night and
Father heard it crash as it hit something.
He waited anxiously for the ladybug to explode,
but nothing happened. Father decided he must have hit
the ladybug and the formula worked, so he went to bed.

The next day, the girls were so sad that the ladybug was gone. Father didn't like seeing his daughters sad, so he gave them money and his formula. The girls opened The Ladybug Museum and they lived happily...

...for now!

Noteworthy:
In the next installment, read about how the Miniature Marvelous Ladybug survives in the New World.

CPSIA information can be obtained
at www.ICGtesting.com
Printed in the USA
LVHW070549010322
712199LV00005BA/97